Cal and Kip

by Alex Yu
illustrated by Kersti Frigell

Core Decodable 23

McGraw Hill Education

Bothell, WA • Chicago, IL • Columbus, OH • New York, NY

MHEonline.com

Send all inquiries to:
McGraw-Hill Education
8787 Orion Place
Columbus, OH 43240

ISBN: 978-0-02-144926-2
MHID: 0-02-144926-0

Printed in Canada.

9 10 11 12 KOD 24

A tall man is on sand.

Bobcats spot the tall man.

Cal and Kip Bobcat talk.

"The sand is hot," said Kip.

The tall man sat on a small rock.

The tall man had a black cap.

"Can I have a cap?" said Cal.

"Bobcats can't have caps," said Kip.

The tall man had a backpack.

"Bobcats can't have backpacks," said Cal.

The tall man had a small snack.

“And Bobcats skip snacks,” said Kip.

The tall man had a sip.

"It's hot," said Cal.

"Sip and drip a lot," said Kip.

The tall man trots past Cal and Kip.